THE Bible Study Guide
FOR BEGINNERS

By Chanté Griffin

chartwell books

Quarto

© 2026 Quarto Publishing Group USA Inc.

This edition published in 2026 by Chartwell Books,
an imprint of The Quarto Group
142 West 36th Street, 4th Floor
New York, NY 10018 USA
T (212) 779-4972
www.Quarto.com

All rights reserved. No part of this book may be reproduced in any form without written permission of the copyright owners. All images in this book have been reproduced with the knowledge and prior consent of the artists concerned, and no responsibility is accepted by producer, publisher, or printer for any infringement of copyright or otherwise, arising from the contents of this publication. Every effort has been made to ensure that credits accurately comply with information supplied. We apologize for any inaccuracies that may have occurred and will resolve inaccurate or missing information in a subsequent reprinting of the book.

10 9 8 7 6 5 4 3 2 1

Chartwell titles are also available at discount for retail, wholesale, promotional, and bulk purchase. For details, contact the Special Sales Manager by email at specialsales@quarto.com or by mail at The Quarto Group, Attn: Special Sales Manager, 100 Cummings Center Suite 265D, Beverly, MA 01915, USA.

ISBN: 978-0-7858-4696-3

Publisher: Wendy Friedman
Publishing Director: Meredith Mennitt
Editor: Joanne O'Sullivan
Designer: Brianna Tong
Image credits: Shutterstock

Printed in China

EEA Representation, WTS Tax d.o.o.,
Žanova ulica 3, 4000 Kranj, Slovenia.
www.wts-tax.si

CONTENTS

INTRODUCTION

THE STRUCTURE OF THE BIBLE

HOW TO USE THIS BOOK

THE OLD TESTAMENT
- Books of the Law
- The Historical Books
- The Poetic Books
- The Prophetic Books

THE NEW TESTAMENT
- The Gospels
- Acts (The Historical Book)
- The Letters
- Revelation (The Book of Vision)

INTRODUCTION

The Bible has sold more copies than any other book in history. Its pages paint a holistic picture of the Judeo-Christian God: his love, character, and promises. Its pages also paint a picture of humanity: our beauty, flaws, and proclivities. Studying the Bible allows you to understand the Judeo-Christian God and the biblical stories that have been told around the globe, from ancient times until today. Studying the Bible also can ignite or strengthen your relationship with the God who inspired its pages.

The Bible Study Guide for Beginners is designed for anyone who's never read the Bible before and those who want to better understand it. Although there are dozens of Bible study methods, the approach taught in this guide is simple and accessible for most people. This study guide helps you study the Bible book-by-book to give you a general overview of the Scriptures. If you read approximately four chapters a day, you can read the entire Bible and complete this guide in about a year.

Those who want to understand and follow the Scriptures should know that studying the Bible well is as necessary as it is challenging. For one, the Bible was written in Hebrew, Greek, and Aramaic. Its translation to English (and other languages) has produced dozens of translations, all of which communicate slightly different meanings. Additionally, there are so many different interpretations of Scripture that there are tens of thousands of Christian denominations throughout the world.

Another challenge is that the Bible is not presented in chronological order. (Don't worry—this guide gives you tools to navigate this.) Scripture study can also be challenging because the Bible is long. This is why studying the Bible over the course of a year works well. You can make a lot of progress if you study just a few chapters each day.

All the challenges are more than worth it, though. In Matthew 13:44-45, Jesus said, "The kingdom of heaven is like treasure hidden in a field. When a man found it, he hid it again, and then in his joy went and sold all he had and bought that field. Again, the kingdom of heaven is like a merchant looking for fine pearls. When he found one of great value, he went away and sold everything he had and bought it."

Jesus was saying that God's kingdom is so valuable that it's worth selling everything for. Living out the Scriptures is how you enter God's kingdom. Considering this, the Scriptures are worth all the time and energy it takes to study them. They are worth the challenge. Parts of the Bible can't be understood simply by reading them once. To truly understand, you have to ask questions and dig deeper. This is why Jesus spoke in parables throughout the Scriptures: so that the mysteries of God's kingdom would be revealed only to those who truly wanted to understand them.

BIBLE FACTS

- 66 books
- Approximately 40 authors
- Two Parts: Old Testament and New Testament
- Original Languages: Hebrew, Greek, Aramaic
- Bible books are referenced by the book's name, followed by the book's chapter number and verse number. Ex. Matthew 1:12 refers to verse twelve of the first chapter of the book of Matthew.

THE STRUCTURE OF THE BIBLE

As a book, the Bible is as literary as it is theological. It contains stories, history, laws, letters, prophecies, and poetry, which all point to how the Gospel is "good news" for creation.

The Bible has different genres, or types of books. Each genre is written differently for a specific purpose. These genres will be discussed later in the guide, but here is a breakdown.

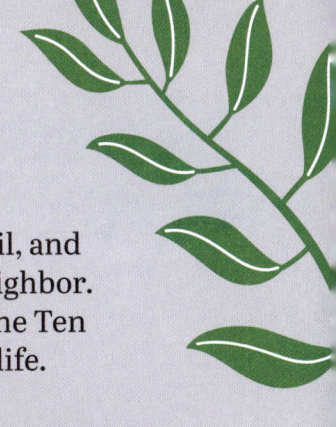

Old Testament

Books of the Law

The Books of the Law contain hundreds of moral, civil, and ceremonial laws for how to interact with God and neighbor. Delivered through Moses, the laws, which included the Ten Commandments, touched on almost every aspect of life.

- Genesis
- Exodus
- Leviticus
- Numbers
- Deuteronomy

> ¹³ Moses answered the people, "Do not be afraid. Stand firm and you will see the deliverance the Lord will bring you today. The Egyptians you see today you will never see again. ¹⁴ The Lord will fight for you; you need only to be still."
>
> **Exodus 14:13-14**

The Historical Books

The Historical Books narrate the story of the Israelites and the fulfillment of God's promises to their patriarchs. The Historical Books record their entrance into the Promised Land, the rise and fall of their kingdom, their exile, and eventual return to their land.

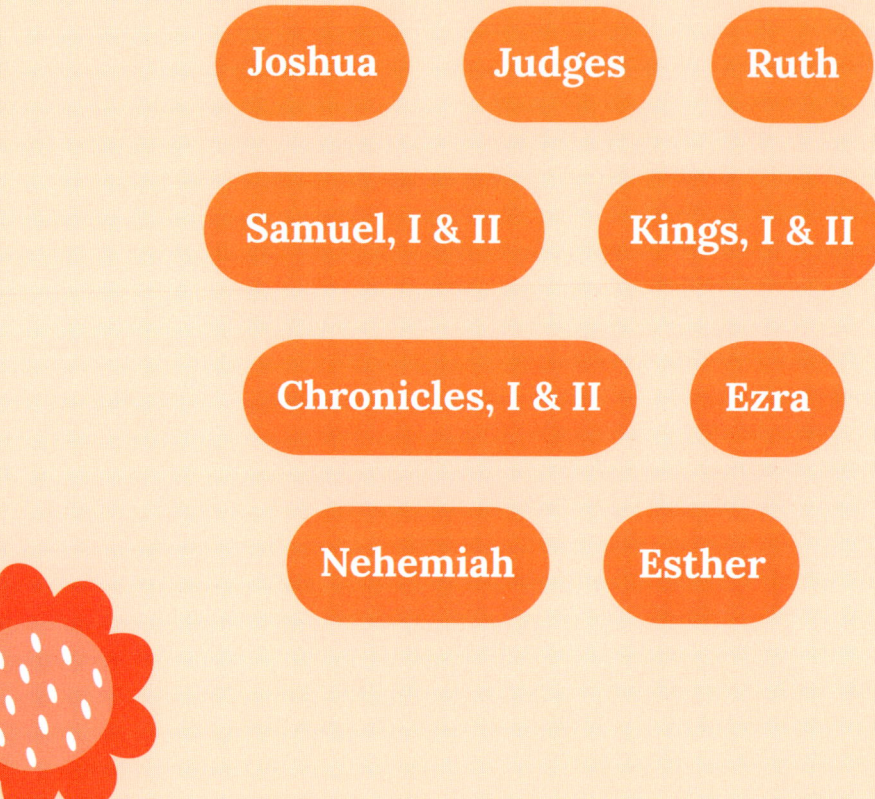

The Poetic Books

The Poetic Books use poetry to beautifully depict life's joys and pains. The books offer ageless wisdom for how to live a good, godly life.

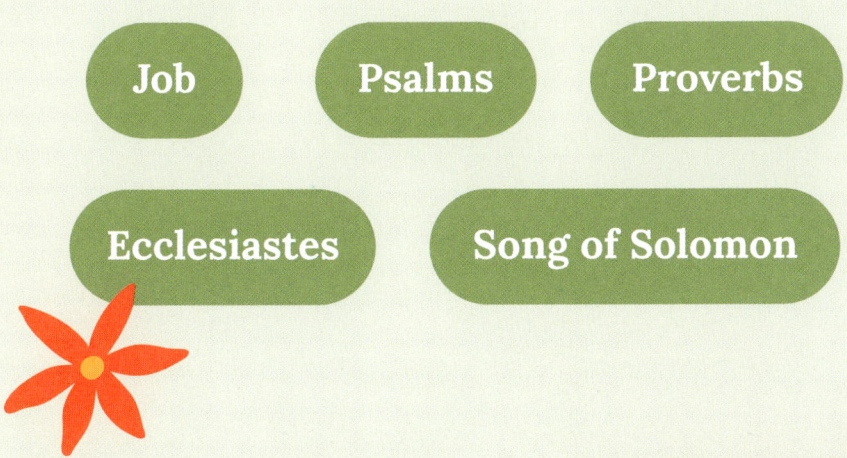

Psalm 100
A psalm. For giving grateful praise.

1 Shout for joy to the Lord, all the earth.

2 Worship the Lord with gladness;
come before him with joyful songs.

3 Know that the Lord is God.
It is he who made us, and we are his[a];
we are his people, the sheep of his pasture.

4 Enter his gates with thanksgiving
and his courts with praise;
give thanks to him and praise his name.

5 For the Lord is good and his love endures forever;
his faithfulness continues through all generations.

The Prophetic Books

The Prophetic Books contain God's messages to the Israelites through the prophets, his chosen messengers. The overriding message of the Prophetic Books is simple: If you are faithful to God's commandments, then you will be blessed. If you are unfaithful, then you will be punished.

Major Prophets

- Isaiah
- Jeremiah
- Lamentations
- Ezekiel
- Daniel

Minor Prophets

- Hosea
- Joel
- Amos
- Obadiah
- Jonah
- Micah
- Nahum
- Habakkuk
- Zephaniah
- Haggai
- Zechariah
- Malachi

New Testament

The Gospels

The Gospels record the life and ministry of Jesus from four different perspectives. Individually and collectively, the Gospels reveal how Jesus is the fulfillment of the Old Testament Law and the Promised Messiah the prophets preached about.

- Matthew
- Mark
- Luke
- John

> In the same way, let your light shine before others, that they may see your good deeds and glorify your Father in heaven.
>
> **Matthew 5:16**

Acts (The Historical Book)

The book of Acts is a Historical Book that documents both how the gospel message spread and how the early church grew. Acts details how the Holy Spirit empowered Christ followers to work through cultural differences and spread the gospel message across the world.

Repent, then, and turn to God, so that your sins may be wiped out, that times of refreshing may come from the Lord.

Acts 3:19

The Letters

Written to churches and individuals, the Letters were penned to bring encouragement, clarity, and correction. The Letters illuminate how Christ's gospel challenges cultural norms, ignites God-honoring suffering, and brings restoration and reconciliation.

- Romans
- Corinthians, I & II
- Galatians
- Ephesians
- Philippians
- Colossians
- Thessalonians, I & II
- Timothy, I & II
- Titus
- Philemon
- Hebrews
- James
- Peter, I & II
- John, I, II, & III
- Jude

Revelation (The Book of Vision)

Revelation is one-of-a-kind. This Book of Vision records the visions God gave to its author, which are prophetic and apocalyptic. Revelation reveals the final events that take place in the world before it ends.

Revelation

BIBLE STUDY RESOURCES

Some of these resources are available in print, while others are available solely online.

BibleProject.org

BibleHub.com

GotQuestions.org

Tyndale Old Testament Commentaries

William Barclay's Daily Study Bible
(New Testament commentary)

InterVarsity Press Bible Dictionary

Strong's Concordance (strongsconcordance.org)

*How to Read the Bible for All Its Worth
by Gordon D. Fee and Douglas Stuart

*Note: this book is a detailed resource that shaped some of the ideas presented throughout this guide.

HOW TO USE THIS BOOK

One of the most common misconceptions about the Bible is that you can just pick it up, read it, and understand what it means *and* how to apply it to your life. That's simply not true. To *truly* understand the Bible, you have to study it. Don't worry if you're not adept at studying or feel rusty because you haven't been in school for a while. Reading ahead, you'll find four simple steps you can take to study the Bible so you understand what it meant when it was written as well as what it means for us today. Also, thankfully there are tons of Bible scholars who have spent decades intensely studying the Bible, and their resources are available for us to read, as needed.

Like the Bible, this guide is divided into two sections: the Old Testament and the New Testament. Within these two sections are genre sections that include a summary of the books within those genres, as well as study questions, tips for reading those books, and blank pages. This guide includes prompts for using the four-step study process for each section of the Bible.

Your Bible Study Process

1. Research

The first step in our Bible Study process is to research each book: its author, genre, setting, historical context, and purpose. (Please note that this research doesn't need to take hours. It can take as little as 15 minutes.) Before you read any book of the Bible, you want to answer the following questions. You can find a Bible study resource that answers these questions for each book of the Bible. There are many reputable study resources, both printed and online. You can also check the list of resources on page 15.

Once you select a resource, answer the following questions:

Book Type
What type of book is it? Historical? Law? Poetic? Gospel? Prophetic? Understanding each book's genre will help you know how best to read it and interpret it.

Historical Context
Briefly research the city/geographic area, its people, their customs, their culture, political context, etc.... to understand the historical context the book was written in.

Who
Who wrote the book? Who is the subject of the book?

When
When was the book written? When did the events described in the book occur?

Where
Where was the book written? Where do the described events take place?

What
What is the book about? What happens within its pages? What are its themes?

Why
Why was this book written? What is its purpose in the biblical canon?

2. Read: Outline and Note

After you've researched the answers to these questions, you want to read through the book, outlining it and noting what stands out to you, as well as what puzzles you.

Read through the book, chapter by chapter, verse by verse. As you read, create an outline of the book. While outlining, be sure to note events, topics, characters, and settings. Some Bibles may offer headers for various chapters and sub-sections, which can be helpful. However, creating your own outline will help you think about the book as a whole unit and better understand its themes. Outlining will also ensure that you read actively. Don't worry, the outline doesn't need to be perfect. The goal is simply to get your mind to engage with the material and to gain a better understanding of the author's intent.

As you outline, write down any observations. An observation is literally anything you want to note. Maybe something surprising or something you want to remember.

Don't forget to note any questions, the things that you don't understand or feel startling. Remember: your discomfort might be the first step to growth and a deeper understanding of God.

3. Revelation

The Bible is God's revelation to us. Biblical 'revelation' simply refers to God's nature and desires being disclosed to us. For this reason, this third section is extremely important.

After you have researched the book and then read and outlined it while noting questions and observations, you should have a basic grasp of the book's structure and themes. At this point you can start to understand what the author is revealing about God. With an open mind and an open heart, you can understand and receive revelation.

When trying to understand what is being revealed about God in a particular book and within different chapters and verses, you always want to ask two questions:

> 1. What did it mean to them (the original audience)?
> 2. What does it mean to us today—and to me?

To answer the first question, *What did it mean to them?*, you can read from a Bible Commentary (see page 15 for resources). This commentary will provide insight on the meanings of the books and their specific chapters and verses.

If you'd like to do a little more digging on your own, then you can look up topics and places in a Bible Dictionary or Bible map (also on the list of resources on page 15). If you want to dig even more, then you can research a specific word in a Bible verse in its original language by using a Bible Concordance.

Answering this first question is crucial because it's only *after* you understand what the book meant to the people it was written to that you can understand what it means to us, collectively today—and to you personally.

When thinking about the second question, *What does it mean to us today—and to me?*, you want to understand what the Scripture is saying to the world and to Christ followers today. Are we being asked to think differently? Are we being asked to act differently? Are we being corrected? Encouraged?

As you read commentary written by Bible scholars to better understand each book, you also want to use your critical thinking skills. You'll find that there is rarely agreement among scholars on *anything* in the Bible, although sometimes there is a general consensus on some topics. Use your mind and your specific questions and notes to aid your study. Also, be sure to ask God to reveal the meaning of Scripture to you as well. One best practice as you study is to pray and ask God to open your heart and your mind to the truth of the Scriptures.

4. Response

The final step in this Bible Study process is your response to the revelation. How will you respond to the truth that's been revealed to you during your study?

When studying the Scriptures, it's important not only to study them, but to allow them to study *you*. Allow their teaching to shape your mind and your heart. Allow God to use the Scriptures to shape your beliefs as well as your actions. In James 1:19-25, we're asked not only to hear the Word, but to actually *do* what it says. It can be argued that *doing* what the Bible says is the most important part of studying the Bible.

How to Read the Bible: Tips

Reading chapters aloud may help you better grasp their themes and message.

When reading the Bible and interpreting specific verses, it's important to never take a verse out of context. Each verse should be interpreted within its historical context *and* its literary context. The verses immediately before and after a verse always inform its meaning, as do the chapters surrounding it.

WHAT DO THE NUMBERS MEAN ON THE VERSES?

The verse numbers in the Bible serve as a navigational tool for reference and study. The Bible originally was presented in unbroken text. The numbers were added in the early thirteenth century, and the verse divisions were in the sixteenth century.

The numbers sometimes interrupt the natural flow of the text. They are not indicative of any inherent meaning within the scripture but rather just to help you find your way in Scripture.

WHAT VERSIONS OF THE BIBLE ARE AVAILABLE?

The Bible has been translated into numerous English versions, each with distinct translation philosophies and purposes. These versions range from formal equivalence (word-for-word) to dynamic equivalence (thought-for-thought), and paraphrased translations. Formal equivalence translations, like the King James Version (KJV) and English Standard Version (ESV), aim for literal accuracy, preserving original language structures. Dynamic equivalence versions, such as the New International Version (NIV) and New Living Translation (NLT), prioritize readability and contemporary language. Paraphrased versions, like The Message (MSG), rephrase texts for modern understanding and devotional reading.

The following chart offers a basic explanation of the different versions and the abbreviations you'll see associated with them.

Abbreviation	Name	Description
KJV	King James Version	1611 translation; known for its majestic language; widely used in Protestant traditions.
NKJV	New King James Version	1982 update of KJV; modernized language while retaining traditional style.
ESV	English Standard Version	2001 translation; formal equivalence; popular among evangelicals.
NIV	New International Version	1978 translation; dynamic equivalence; balances accuracy and readability.
NLT	New Living Translation	1996 translation; dynamic equivalence; emphasizes clarity for modern readers.
NASB	New American Standard Bible	1971 translation; formal equivalence; known for literal accuracy.
NRSV	New Revised Standard Version	1989 translation; formal equivalence; widely accepted in academic and liturgical settings.
CEV	Contemporary English Version	1995 translation; dynamic equivalence; designed for clarity and simplicity.
ASV	American Standard Version	1901 translation; formal equivalence; predecessor to NASB.
RSV	Revised Standard Version	1952 translation; formal equivalence; bridge between KJV and modern translations.
RNJB	Revised New Jerusalem Bible	2019 Catholic translation; formal equivalence; successor to the Jerusalem Bible.
MSG	The Message	2002 paraphrase; contemporary language; focuses on conveying the essence of passages.

THE OLD TESTAMENT

Books of The Law

OLD TESTAMENT

BOOKS OF THE LAW

Genesis
Exodus
Leviticus
Numbers
Deuteronomy

The Books of the Law, also known as the Pentateuch or Torah, are the first five books of the Old Testament. Testament means "covenant," so the Old Testament is the Old Covenant God made with his chosen people. These first five books detail the more than six hundred laws God gave them to live by. Moses has been credited as their author, but some Bible scholars question his authorship.

Intertwined with these laws are narratives about how God created humankind and the Earth; stories about how sin separated God from his good creation; and stories about God's plan to redeem all of his creation. Biblical narratives tell many interconnected stories: the meta-narrative of God's plan for creation and people, God's redemption of his people through the Old Covenant and the New Covenant, and the individual stories of how people and nations responded to these covenants.

The Books of the Law depict a good and holy God who continuously invites humankind into his goodness but is rejected repeatedly through sin and rebellion. The books show a loving God who continuously extends grace because he wants to bless and live in communion with his creation.

In addition to revealing the creation story, Genesis introduces Abram, who will be renamed "Abraham" which means father of many. Genesis 12:1-2 sets up the Bible's redemption story: "The Lord had said to Abram, 'Go from your country, your people and your father's household to the land I will show you. I will make you into a great nation, and I will bless you; I will make your name great, and you will be a blessing.'" Genesis also introduces Abraham's son, Isaac, and his son, Jacob, who is renamed "Israel." Later in Genesis we see God saving the children of Israel through Abraham's great-grandson Joseph. Joseph welcomes his entire family into a prospering Egypt during a worldwide famine they would not have survived otherwise.

Exodus narrates how the children of Israel grew in Egypt, only to be persecuted and enslaved by the new Pharaoh who feared their growing numbers. Exodus recounts Moses' story of adoption and eventual leadership of the Israelites out of slavery into "the Promised Land." The book shows God giving the Ten Commandments at Mt. Sinai and instructions for the tabernacle where his presence could dwell among them. Lastly, Exodus shows the people rebel against God by making idols.

The book of Leviticus focuses on how the Israelites can live as God's chosen people, in God's presence, despite their perpetual sin. Leviticus lays out exactly how their sin must be atoned for so they can stand before a sinless, holy God. The book lists the ritual feasts and sacrifices to be upheld. Priests, who are held to the highest standards, are ordained so they can serve in the tabernacle, making atonement for the people's sin. God repeatedly reminds the Israelites that they must live differently than the people in the land He's sending them into. "I am the LORD, who brought you up out of Egypt to be your God; therefore, be holy, because I am holy" (Leviticus 11:45).

In the book of Numbers, the children of Israel are counted in a census. The book narrates their travel through the wilderness on their way to the promised land of Canaan. Twelve spies from the twelves tribes are sent out to scout the land. Some return with positive reports about the land while others, ladened with fear, report otherwise. Disbelief permeates their hearts and minds, and as a result God says they will not see the Promised Land; They will wander in the wilderness (Numbers 14).

Deuteronomy begins with Moses teaching the new generation of Israelites to be faithful to the covenant. "Hear, Israel, and be careful to obey so that it may go well with you and that you may increase greatly in a land flowing with milk and honey, just as the LORD, the God of your ancestors, promised you. Hear, O Israel: The LORD our God, the LORD is one. Love the LORD your God with all your heart and with all your soul and with all your strength" (Deuteronomy 6:3-5).

In this book, they are on the precipice of what God promised their forefather Abraham many years before. As they settle into a new land, God wants them to be devoted solely to him and his ways. Moses gives additional laws related to worship, family life, and civic life. The least among them (widows, orphans, immigrants) should be cared for.

A study of the Historical Books (pages 50 to 67) will reveal whether or not they heeded the instructions God gave through Moses.

How to Read the Books of the Law

The law books detail the lineage of Abraham, the father of the Christian faith. Finding a family tree that starts with Abraham and ends with Jesus will help you better understand the meta-narratives and individual stories told throughout the law books and the rest of the Bible. (Note: You can find one online.)

Be sure to read these Old Testament narratives as descriptive narratives, rather than prescriptive narratives. In other words, they aren't necessarily designed to teach us how to live, but rather how the people within its pages lived.

PASSAGES TO PONDER

Genesis 1 – [1] In the beginning God created the heavens and the earth. [2] Now the earth was formless and empty, darkness was over the surface of the deep, and the Spirit of God was hovering over the waters.

[3] And God said, "Let there be light," and there was light. [4] God saw that the light was good, and he separated the light from the darkness. [5] God called the light "day," and the darkness he called "night." And there was evening, and there was morning—the first day.

[6] And God said, "Let there be a vault between the waters to separate water from water." [7] So God made the vault and separated the water under the vault from the water above it. And it was so. [8] God called the vault "sky." And there was evening, and there was morning—the second day.

[9] And God said, "Let the water under the sky be gathered to one place, and let dry ground appear." And it was so. [10] God called the dry ground "land," and the gathered waters he called "seas." And God saw that it was good.

[11] Then God said, "Let the land produce vegetation: seed-bearing plants and trees on the land that bear fruit with seed in it, according to their various kinds." And it was so. [12] The land produced vegetation: plants bearing seed according to their kinds and trees bearing fruit with seed in it according to their kinds. And God saw that it was good. [13] And there was evening, and there was morning—the third day.

[14] And God said, "Let there be lights in the vault of the sky to separate the day from the night, and let them serve as signs to mark sacred times, and days and years, [15] and let them be lights in the vault of the sky to give light on the earth." And it was so. [16] God made two great lights—the greater light to govern the day and the lesser light to govern the night. He also made the stars. [17] God set them in the vault of the sky to give light on the earth, [18] to govern the day and the night, and to separate light from darkness. And God saw that it was good. [19] And there was evening, and there was morning—the fourth day.

[20] And God said, "Let the water teem with living creatures, and let birds fly above the earth across the vault of the sky." [21] So God created the great creatures of the sea and every living thing with which the water teems and that moves about in it, according to their kinds, and every winged bird according to its kind. And God saw that it was good. [22] God blessed them and said, "Be fruitful and increase in number and fill the water in the seas, and let the birds increase on the earth." [23] And there was evening, and there was morning—the fifth day.

[24] And God said, "Let the land produce living creatures according to their kinds: the livestock, the creatures that move along the ground, and the wild animals, each according to its kind." And it was so. [25] God made the wild animals according to their kinds, the livestock according to their kinds, and all the creatures that move along the ground according to their kinds. And God saw that it was good.

²⁶ Then God said, "Let us make mankind in our image, in our likeness, so that they may rule over the fish in the sea and the birds in the sky, over the livestock and all the wild animals,[a] and over all the creatures that move along the ground."

²⁷ So God created mankind in his own image,
    in the image of God he created them;
    male and female he created them.

²⁸ God blessed them and said to them, "Be fruitful and increase in number; fill the earth and subdue it. Rule over the fish in the sea and the birds in the sky and over every living creature that moves on the ground."

²⁹ Then God said, "I give you every seed-bearing plant on the face of the whole earth and every tree that has fruit with seed in it. They will be yours for food. ³⁰ And to all the beasts of the earth and all the birds in the sky and all the creatures that move along the ground—everything that has the breath of life in it—I give every green plant for food." And it was so.

³¹ God saw all that he had made, and it was very good. And there was evening, and there was morning—the sixth day.

Genesis 2:1-3 – [1] Thus the heavens and the earth were completed in all their vast array.

[2] By the seventh day God had finished the work he had been doing; so on the seventh day he rested from all his work. [3] Then God blessed the seventh day and made it holy, because on it he rested from all the work of creating that he had done.

Deuteronomy 6:4-9 – [4] Hear, O Israel: The Lord our God, the Lord is one.[a] [5] Love the Lord your God with all your heart and with all your soul and with all your strength. [6] These commandments that I give you today are to be on your hearts. [7] Impress them on your children. Talk about them when you sit at home and when you walk along the road, when you lie down and when you get up. [8] Tie them as symbols on your hands and bind them on your foreheads. [9] Write them on the doorframes of your houses and on your gates.

Exodus 20:1–17 – And God spoke these words: ² I am the Lord your God, who brought you out of Egypt, out of the land of slavery.

³ You shall have no other gods before[a] me.

⁴ You shall not make for yourself an image in the form of anything in heaven above or on the earth beneath or in the waters below. ⁵ You shall not bow down to them or worship them; for I, the Lord your God, am a jealous God, punishing the children for the sin of the parents to the third and fourth generation of those who hate me, ⁶ but showing love to a thousand generations of those who love me and keep my commandments.

⁷ You shall not misuse the name of the Lord your God, for the Lord will not hold anyone guiltless who misuses his name.

⁸ Remember the Sabbath day by keeping it holy. ⁹ Six days you shall labor and do all your work, ¹⁰ but the seventh day is a sabbath to the Lord your God. On it you shall not do any work, neither you, nor your son or daughter, nor your male or female servant, nor your animals, nor any foreigner residing in your towns. ¹¹ For in six days the Lord made the heavens and the earth, the sea, and all that is in them, but he rested on the seventh day. Therefore, the Lord blessed the Sabbath day and made it holy.

¹² Honor your father and your mother, so that you may live long in the land the Lord your God is giving you.

¹³ You shall not murder.

¹⁴ You shall not commit adultery.

¹⁵ You shall not steal.

¹⁶ You shall not give false testimony against your neighbor.

¹⁷ You shall not covet your neighbor's house. You shall not covet your neighbor's wife, or his male or female servant, his ox or donkey, or anything that belongs to your neighbor.

Bible Study Process

† Who wrote these books? Who are the subjects of these books?

_____
_____
_____
_____
_____
_____
_____
_____
_____
_____
_____

† What type of books are these?

_____
_____
_____
_____
_____
_____
_____
_____
_____
_____
_____

† When were these books written?

† When did the events described in the books occur?

† Where were these books written? Where do the described events take place?

† What was the historical context for these books?

† What happens within the pages of these books? What are their themes?

† Why were these books written? What are their purposes in the biblical canon?

† What did these books mean to the original audience?

† What do these books mean to us today—and to me?

† How will you respond to the truth that's been revealed to you during your study?

Study Questions

† What are the terms of the covenant that God makes with his people?

† What do we learn about God's character considering the covenant he makes with Abraham, despite Abraham's shortcomings?

† What are the different categories of laws and why were they included?

† It's impossible to follow six hundred laws, so why did God make so many?

† How does God show love to his people in these books, and how do they respond in return?

The Historical Books

THE HISTORICAL BOOKS

Joshua
Judges
Ruth
Samuel, I & II
Kings, I & II
Chronicles, I & II
Ezra
Nehemiah
Esther

The Historical Books document the Israelites' time in the Promised Land—from their initial arrival and appointment of ruling judges and kings—to the kingdom's split, their exile out of the land, and their eventual return. The Historical Books highlight their repeating cycles of sin, its consequences, their repentance, and their deliverance. By recounting the missteps and sinful tendencies of the Israelites and their priests, judges, and kings, these books reveal that the people are capable neither of being faithful to God nor of leading themselves. In this sense, the books point to the need for a messianic king.

The book of Joshua recounts the battles the Israelites fought to receive the land God had promised them and how they adopted the sinful practices of the Canaanites after they settled into the land. In the book of Judges, God appointed judges to govern the Israelites, including a female judge named Deborah. "Yet they would not listen to their judges but prostituted themselves to other gods and worshiped them. They quickly turned from the ways of their ancestors, who had been obedient to the LORD's commands" (Judges 2:17). At the end of Judges, the author foreshadowed what was to come: "In those days Israel had no king; everyone did as he saw fit" (Judges 21:25).

1 and 2 Samuel recount the miraculous birth story of the prophet Samuel, and the books show the Israelites finally get what they've wanted—a king. The reign of their first leader, King Saul, starts off well, but ends with Saul in a maddened state trying to murder David, his successor. When David takes the throne, he's humble with a heart that is faithful to God. But his kingship takes a turn after he engages in adultery and murder (2 Samuel 11). Afterward, in a twisted turn of events, one of his sons tries to murder him to ascend to the throne. Throughout it all, God promises to fulfill his promise to bring a messiah through David's line: "Your house and your kingdom will endure forever before me your throne will be established forever" (2 Samuel 7:16).

1 & 2 Kings continue where 2 Samuel ends. Solomon takes the throne after David, then builds the temple of God in Jerusalem, as written in 1 Chronicles 28:5. "Of all my sons—and the LORD has given me many—he has chosen my son Solomon to sit on the throne of the kingdom of the LORD over Israel." But Solomon's devotion is split: he also marries foreign women and eventually begins to worship their gods. In yet another turn of events, Solomon's son, Rehoboam rebels and splits the kingdom. His kingdom becomes known as the Northern Kingdom, Israel, and he builds another temple there. Meanwhile Solomon reigns over the Southern Kingdom, Judah, which houses the true temple in Jerusalem. 1 & 2 Kings end with the destruction of both kingdoms and the exile of the Israelites from their land.

1 & 2 Chronicles are unique because they do not pick up where 1 & 2 Kings end. Instead, 1 & 2 Chronicles retell the stories told in 1 & 2 Kings and 1 & 2 Samuel, with repeated and expanded details.

Ruth and Esther are unique books because they are named after women—their protagonists—and because they show God bringing salvation and deliverance to the Israelites through these women. In Ruth, a Moabite woman named Ruth refuses to leave her Israelite mother-in-law after Ruth's husband dies. Instead, she tells her mother-in-law, Naomi, "Where you go I will go, and where you stay, I will stay. Your people will be my people and your God my God" (Ruth 1:16b). The two find a "kinsman redeemer" named Boaz to marry Ruth, care for them, and restore their family line. Ruth and Boaz have a son and become a part of the genealogical line of King David and Jesus.

In the book of Esther, Esther is a young Jewish woman living with the Israelites in exile. Through a series of events, she marries King Ahasuerus. She puts her life on the line to save her people, who are threatened with death. A woman of faith, she tells her advisor, Mordecai: "Go, gather together all the Jews who are in Susa, and fast for me. Do not eat or drink for three days, night or day. I and my attendants will fast as you do. When this is done, I will go to the king, even though it is against the law. And if I perish, I perish" (Esther 4:16b).

Ezra and Nehemiah, originally written as one book, "Ezra-Nehemiah," record how some of the Israelites return to their land after exile. Three central figures lead the restoration. Zerubbabel rebuilds the temple in Jerusalem (Ezra 1-6), Ezra teaches the law to those returning (Ezra 7-10), and Nehemiah rebuilds the wall that surrounds Jerusalem. By the end of Nehemiah, while the physical restoration of the temple and the city have taken place, the hearts of the people are still far from God.

How to Read the Historical Books

The Historical Books cover extended periods of time, sometimes repeat events, and are not presented in chronological order. To clearly understand the timeline of each book, it's suggested that you access a timeline. You can find one by using one of the resources listed on page 15 of this book. Another option is type "Timeline of Bible kingdoms and kings" or "Timeline of Bible prophets" into an online search to find one to aid your study.

The Historical Books also document travel across different regions. To better understand where the stories take place, you either can use one of the recommended resources or search online for a "map of the Old Testament."

PASSAGES TO PONDER

Joshua 1:5 – No one will be able to stand against you... I will never leave you nor forsake you." A powerful reassurance of God's faithful presence.

Joshua 1:9 – Have I not commanded you? Be strong and courageous. Do not be afraid; do not be discouraged, for the Lord your God will be with you wherever you go.

Ruth 1:16–17 – But Ruth replied, "Don't urge me to leave you or to turn back from you. Where you go, I will go, and where you stay, I will stay. Your people will be my people and your God my God. ¹⁷ Where you die, I will die, and there I will be buried. May the Lord deal with me, be it ever so severely, if even death separates you and me."

1 Samuel 16:7 – But the Lord said to Samuel, "Do not consider his appearance or his height, for I have rejected him. The Lord does not look at the things people look at. People look at the outward appearance, but the Lord looks at the heart."

2 Chronicles 7:14 – If my people, who are called by my name, will humble themselves and pray and seek my face and turn from their wicked ways, then I will hear from heaven, and I will forgive their sin and will heal their land.

1 Kings 2:3 – And observe what the LORD your God requires: Walk in obedience to him, and keep his decrees and commands, his laws and regulations, as written in the Law of Moses. Do this so that you may prosper in all you do and wherever you go.

Nehemiah 9:10 – You sent signs and wonders against Pharaoh, against all his officials and all the people of his land, for you knew how arrogantly the Egyptians treated them. You made a name for yourself, which remains to this day.

Bible Study Process

† Who wrote these books? Who are the subjects of these books?

___

___

___

___

___

___

___

___

___

___

† What type of books are these?

___

___

___

___

___

___

___

___

___

___

† When were these books written?

† When did the events described in the books occur?

† Where were these books written? Where do the described events take place?

_____
_____
_____
_____
_____
_____
_____
_____
_____
_____

† What was the historical context for these books?

_____
_____
_____
_____
_____
_____
_____
_____
_____
_____

† What happens within the pages of these books? What are their themes?

† Why were these books written? What are their purposes in the biblical canon?

† What did these books mean to the original audience?

_____
_____
_____
_____
_____
_____
_____
_____
_____
_____
_____
_____

† What do these books mean to us today—and to me?

_____
_____
_____
_____
_____
_____
_____
_____
_____
_____
_____
_____

† How will you respond to the truth that's been revealed to you during your study?

Study Questions

† Why do the Israelites repeatedly worship the gods of the neighboring nations instead of staying true to the covenant?

† What are the roles of the priests, prophets, judges, and kings in these books, and why did God appoint them?

† What does the temple in Jerusalem symbolize, and what is the significance of its destruction and rebuilding?

† 1 & 2 Corinthians repeat the stories in 1 & 2 Samuel and 1 & 2 Kings. Why do you think these stories were repeated? What's different about the accounts?

† What does the inclusion of stories about Ruth, Esther, Deborah (Judges 4-5), Rahab (Joshua 2-6), and other women in The Historical Books reveal about women's societal roles in ancient Israel and the roles they played in the coming of Jesus, the eternal King?

The Poetic Books

THE POETIC BOOKS

- **Job**
- **Psalms**
- **Proverbs**
- **Ecclesiastes**
- **Song of Songs (Song of Solomon)**

As their name implies, the Poetic Books are all filled with poetry, not unlike many of the Prophetic Books. But the Poetic Books are also known as 'wisdom books,' because of the rich wisdom housed within their poetry. Written by 'wise' men and women (respected members of society who hold positions of power), 'wisdom literature' was common in ancient cultures, offering guidance about life's big questions. These books reflect the time in which they were written, offering timeless insight that's still relevant today. An overarching theme of the Poetic Books is this: "The fear of the LORD is the beginning of wisdom, and knowledge of the Holy One is understanding" (Proverbs 9:10).

Written primarily by King David, Asaph (a poet and musician), and the sons of Korah, the Psalms are a collection of hymns and prayers, written either about God or to God. The Psalms are expressions of the range of human emotion. The Psalms are poems—musical poems—that were sung by singers as worship in the temple. Although there are various types of poems in the Psalms, two of the most common are poems of praise and poems of lament. Two examples include Psalm 19:1b: "The heavens declare the glory of God; the skies proclaim the work of his hands;" and Psalm 22:13: "Roaring lions that tear their prey open their mouths wide against me."

King Solomon, the wisest man in ancient Israel, is credited by some scholars as the author of Proverbs. The Proverbs are memorable, pithy statements that speak truths about various aspects of life including family, work, forgiveness, debt, sex, and alcohol. The Proverbs present general truths designed to help its readers cultivate lives defined by wisdom and faithfulness to God. The Proverbs sometimes seem deceptively easy to interpret, but like all the Poetic Books and all Scripture, they are best understood through their historical context and original meaning for their original audience. Like the other Poetic Books, Proverbs is filled with numerous literary techniques.

Like the Psalms and Proverbs, Job, Ecclesiastes, and Song of Songs are one-of-a-kind books in the biblical canon. The book of Job, penned by an unknown writer, describes the harrowing story of a non-Israelite named Job who lived in Uz. Satan kills and destroys everyone and everything Job loves, and the book chronicles Job's conversations with his friends and with God. Job asks questions that has troubled countless generations: Why does God allow suffering to happen to good people? Is their suffering proof that God doesn't exist or evidence that He just doesn't care?

Some scholars credit Solomon as the author of Ecclesiastes. Throughout the book, readers hear the words of the Teacher. The book begins with a saying it has become famous for: "'Meaningless! Meaningless!' says the Teacher. 'Utterly meaningless! Everything is meaningless'" (Ecclesiastes 1:2). The book laments the fact that life and all human aspirations and accomplishments are like vapors: fleeting and soon gone. However, at the end of the book, the author declares another, larger truth. "Now all has been heard; here is the conclusion of the matter: Fear God and keep his commandments, for this is the duty of all mankind" (Ecclesiastes 12:13). Following God, the author asserts, is the only lasting, worthwhile human pursuit.

Song of Songs, also known as Song of Solomon, is a collection of love poems credited to Solomon. The title 'Song of Songs' asserts that the poetry is the greatest of all songs. In it we hear from two voices, two married lovers. Their love is fierce, defined by commitment, passion, and desire. "Your breasts are like two fawns, like twin fawns of a gazelle that browse among the lilies" (Song of Songs 4:5). Song of Songs also captures the power of romantic love. "Place me like a seal over your heart, like a seal on your arm; for love is as strong as death, its jealousy unyielding as the grave. It burns like blazing fire, like a mighty flame" (Song of Songs 8:6). Some scholars believe that the book is an allegory for Israel and God, while other scholars believe it's an allegory for the Church and Christ. However one reads it, the book is a poetic, rapt description of deep love and connection.

How to Read the Poetic Books

It's important to read the Poetic Books as literature. Identifying its literary devices (metaphors, hyperbole) as well as its poetic devices (parallelisms, allegories, acrostics, alliteration) will help you understand the true meaning of the Poetic Books.

The Psalms alone are filled with more than a hundred Hebrew poems. Research the different styles of poems presented throughout the Poetic Books. When you read, identity the type of poem and its structure to understand how best to interpret it.

When interpreting meaning within these books, be sure to think about a verse within the context of its chapter and to think about each chapter within the context of the entire book. This will ensure that you glean the proper understanding of specific verses.

PASSAGES TO PONDER

Job 19:25–26 – I know that my redeemer lives, and that in the end he will stand on the earth.

And after my skin has been destroyed, yet in my flesh I will see God.

Psalms 121 – I lift up my eyes to the hills; my help comes from the LORD. He who keeps you will not slumber. The LORD will keep you from all evil.

Psalms 23 – A psalm of David.

[1] The Lord is my shepherd, I lack nothing.
[2] He makes me lie down in green pastures,
he leads me beside quiet waters,
[3] he refreshes my soul.
He guides me along the right paths
for his name's sake.
[4] Even though I walk
through the darkest valley,[a]
I will fear no evil,
for you are with me;
your rod and your staff,
they comfort me.
[5] You prepare a table before me
in the presence of my enemies.
You anoint my head with oil;
my cup overflows.
[6] Surely your goodness and love will follow me
all the days of my life,
and I will dwell in the house of the Lord
forever.

Ecclesiastes 3:1-8 – There is a time for everything, and a season for every activity under the heavens:
² a time to be born and a time to die,
a time to plant and a time to uproot,
³ a time to kill and a time to heal,
a time to tear down and a time to build,
⁴ a time to weep and a time to laugh,
a time to mourn and a time to dance,
⁵ a time to scatter stones and a time to gather them,
a time to embrace and a time to refrain from embracing,
⁶ a time to search and a time to give up,
a time to keep and a time to throw away,
⁷ a time to tear and a time to mend,
a time to be silent and a time to speak,
⁸ a time to love and a time to hate,
a time for war and a time for peace.

Bible Study Process

† Who wrote these books? Who are the subjects of these books?

† What type of books are these?

† When were these books written?

† When did the events described in the books occur?

† Where were these books written? Where do the described events take place?

_____
_____
_____
_____
_____
_____
_____
_____
_____
_____

† What was the historical context for these books?

_____
_____
_____
_____
_____
_____
_____
_____
_____
_____
_____
_____

† What happens within the pages of these books? What are their themes?

† Why were these books written? What are their purposes in the biblical canon?

† What did these books mean to the original audience?

_____
_____
_____
_____
_____
_____
_____
_____
_____
_____
_____

† What do these books mean to us today—and to me?

_____
_____
_____
_____
_____
_____
_____
_____
_____
_____
_____

† How will you respond to the truth that's been revealed to you during your study?

Study Questions

† Can you identify the different types of psalms and give an example of each?

† Poems of lament are prevalent in Psalms. Why are these types of poems so prevalent and what do you notice about their structure?

† According to the book of Proverbs, how can a person obtain and exercise wisdom?

_____
_____
_____
_____
_____
_____
_____
_____
_____
_____

† According to the book of Job, why do righteous people suffer?

_____
_____
_____
_____
_____
_____
_____
_____
_____
_____

† What's the best way to interpret the writer of Ecclesiastes' statement that everything is 'meaningless' considering the advice given in the other wisdom books?

† Why is the Song of Songs in the Bible? Is it an allegory?

The Prophetic Books

OLD TESTAMENT

THE PROPHETIC BOOKS

The Major Prophets
Isaiah
Jeremiah
Lamentations
Ezekiel
Daniel

The Major Prophets

The Prophetic Books in the Old Testament were written by prophets in Israel between approximately 760 and 460 BCE. In the Bible, prophets were God's spokespeople. Per their title, they sometimes spoke about future events, but they usually spoke about the children of Israel's covenant with God and whether they were being faithful or unfaithful to the covenant. The prophets spoke of the blessings that would come from following the covenant and the punishment that would come from neglecting it.

By 760 BCE, the nation of Israel had been engaged in a longstanding civil war between the northern tribes called 'Israel' or 'Ephraim' and the southern tribes known as Judah. As a result, prophetic books were written either to the Northern Kingdom, to Judah, or to those exiled after the kingdoms were destroyed. (The Northern kingdom was destroyed in 722 BCE and Judah was destroyed in 586 BCE.)

The Prophetic Books consist of the writings of the 'major' prophets (Isaiah, Jeremiah, Ezekiel, Daniel) and twelve 'minor' prophets, also known as "The Twelve." The major and minor prophets hold equal importance. 'Major' simply refers to the longer books, whereas 'minor' refers to the shorter books. Long or short, the Prophetic Books are filled with vivid imagery, memorable metaphors, and easy-to-remember poetry—all of which was essential for generations that relied on shared stories and oral history for learning. When reading the prophets—major and minor—look out for the meaning of the rich imagery, especially to images and language introduced in the law and historical books.

Isaiah prophesied mostly to the Kingdom of Judah. He warned that their unfaithfulness would result in Jerusalem being destroyed by its neighbors; and that the injustice done by neighboring nations would result in their destruction as well. Isaiah also wrote about the hope that would eventually come through the Messiah after the destruction and exile. "For to us a child is born, to us a son is given, and the government will be on his shoulders. And he will be called Wonderful Counselor, Mighty God, Everlasting Father, Prince of Peace" (Isaiah 9:6).

Like Isaiah, Jeremiah rebuked the Kingdom of Judah for breaking the covenant. He warned that they would be destroyed by Babylon if they failed to repent and that God would also judge Babylon. But the prophecy didn't end there; it spoke of a new covenant that God would bring, post-exile. "This is the covenant I will make with the people of Israel after that time," declares the LORD. "I will put my law in their minds and write it on their hearts. I will be their God, and they will be my people" (Jeremiah 31:33).

The prophet Ezekiel was among those in Jerusalem who were taken captive by Babylon. He wrote about Israel's sin and the destruction of the temple. The book is filled with riveting images, including natural disasters—an earthquake and fire—and a valley of dry bones. However, God promises to build a new temple and a new Jerusalem with a new name. "And the name of the city from that time on will be: THE LORD IS THERE" (Ezekiel 48:35b).

The book of Lamentations reads a lot like Psalms. It's composed of poetry, but the poems are laments. The book consists of five poems, four of which are acrostic (alphabet) poems. Some scholars categorize Lamentations as a poetic book, while others categorize it as a prophetic book because the authorship is sometimes attributed to Jeremiah. In the book, the writer laments the invasion and destruction of Jerusalem. He grieves over the people's unfaithfulness and God's punishment of that unfaithfulness. "Her foes have become her master's; her enemies are at ease. The LORD has brought her grief because of her many sins. Her children have gone into exile, captive before the foe" (Lamentations 1:5).

Daniel, the last major prophet, was written after Nebuchadnezzar King of Babylon conquered Judah and took its people into exile.

The book describes how Daniel's faithfulness to God was tested as he served in Nebuchadnezzar's royal court, and how God protected Daniel because of his faithfulness. Daniel told the King of Babylon: "If we are thrown into the blazing furnace, the God we serve can deliver us from it, and he will deliver us from Your Majesty's hand. But even if he does not, we want you to know, Your Majesty, that we will not serve your gods or worship the image of gold you have set up" (Daniel 3:17-18). The book also describes Daniel's dreams and visions about Nebuchadnezzar's pride and the end times.

Although as a genre the Prophetic Books are the most difficult Bible books to comprehend, they can be understood more easily by noting the literary form of each book, its historical context, its audience, and by utilizing Bible study resources. It's crucial to note also that many of the longer, major prophets aren't necessarily cohesive books. Rather, they are compilations of spoken prophecies gathered into singular books.

HOW TO READ THE MAJOR PROPHETS

Before you read each book in the Major Prophets, be sure to understand its audience, historical context, and literary form. Grab a Bible commentary and Bible dictionary that details each book to understand what to look for before you start to read.

Since the Prophetic Books are not presented in chronological order, it may be helpful to locate a timeline of Israel and Judah's captivity and exile to clearly understand the sequence of events the prophets wrote about. An internet search with the words "timeline of Israel's captivity and exile" or "timeline of the Old Testament prophets" will yield some solid resources.

THE PROPHETIC BOOKS

The Minor Prophets
Hosea
Joel
Amos
Obadiah
Jonah
Micah
Nahum
Habakkuk
Zephaniah
Haggai
Zechariah
Malachi

The Minor Prophets

The Minor Prophets of the Old Testament, also known as "The Twelve," are short yet powerful books. Collectively and individually, they show God's correction and covenantal love for the children of Israel, and by extension—all who choose to put their faith in God. The Minor Prophets can be divided into four groups: 1) prophecies to the Northern Kingdom (Israel) 2) prophecies to the Southern Kingdom (Judah) 3) prophecies to all the people, post-exile and 4) other prophecies. Like the Major Prophets, many of the Minor Prophets warned of a coming 'Day of the Lord' that would bring judgement and justice to the nation of Israel and the world. Major themes in these books, often expressed through poetry, include idolatry, adultery, injustice, judgement, captivity, justice, and restoration.

Hosea and Amos were the first prophets to warn the Northern Kingdom of Israel about the impending destruction that would come through Assyria due to Israel's sin. Israel's offenses were many, including worshiping idols and neglecting the poor. In the book of Hosea, God instructed Hosea to marry Gomer, an adulterer, and to restore his relationship with her to illustrate God's commitment to restoring his relationship with Israel, despite its adultery with other gods. Like Hosea, the prophet Amos chastised the people for their duplicitous worship. "Away with the noise of your songs! I will not listen to the music of your harps. But let justice roll on like a river, righteousness like a never-failing stream!" (Amos 5:23-24).

Joel, Micah, Nahum, Habakkuk, and Zephaniah prophesied to the Southern Kingdom of Judah. Micah warned Judah that Assyria and Babylon would overtake the Northern and Southern Kingdoms, but that Assyria would fall as well. After Micah, the prophet Nahum also spoke about the fall of Assyria and its capital, Nineveh, saying, "I am against you," declares the LORD Almighty" (Nahum 2:13a). Habakkuk and Zephaniah prophesied in the final decades before Judah was exiled. These two prophets spoke about the punishments for Judah and its neighbor, Babylon. But Zephaniah also spoke about the potential for future restoration. "Seek the LORD, all you humble of the land, you who do what he commands. Seek righteousness, seek humility; perhaps you will be sheltered on the day of the LORD's anger" (Zephaniah 2:3).

Haggai, Zechariah, and Malachi spoke to the Israelites post-exile, when some had returned to Jerusalem. These three prophets spoke about the physical restoration of God's temple and the spiritual restoration of God's people. Haggai warned them to prioritize their spiritual restoration, which was linked to the physical restoration of the temple. "Is it a time for you yourselves to be living in your paneled houses, while this house remains a ruin?" (Haggai 1:4). Like Haggai, the prophet Zechariah also implored the people to be restored to their God. "Therefore, tell the people: This is what the LORD Almighty says: 'Return to me,' declares the LORD Almighty, 'and I will return to you,' says the LORD Almighty" (Zechariah 1:3).

The books of Obadiah and Jonah don't fit into neat categories because of their uniqueness. Obadiah is the shortest prophetic book, with only twenty-one verses. In it, the prophet speaks against the nation of Edom, the descendants of Esau, for how they helped Babylon destroy Israel. In verse 15 Obadiah proclaims, "The day of the LORD is near for all nations. As you have done, it will be done to you; your deeds will return upon your own head."

The book of Jonah stands alone because its protagonist is Jonah, a wayward prophet who refuses to preach a message of repentance to Israel's enemies in Nineveh (Assyria). Wanting his enemies to be punished by God, Jonah runs away, only to end up in the belly of a big fish for refusing to preach. Eventually he repents and preaches to Nineveh, which results in repentance. God's willingness and desire to forgive all—even his enemies—is clear throughout this book. "When God saw what they did and how they turned from their evil ways, he relented and did not bring on them the destruction he had threatened" (Jonah 3:10).

The message of the Minor Prophets is generally the same, regardless of when, where, or to whom they preached. "Who is a God like you, who pardons sin and forgives the transgression of the remnant of his inheritance? You do not stay angry forever but delight to show mercy. You will again have compassion on us; you will tread our sins underfoot and hurl all our iniquities into the depths of the sea. You will be faithful to Jacob, and show love to Abraham, as you pledged on oath to our ancestors in days long ago" (Micah 7:18-20).

How to Read the Minor Prophets

Before you read each book in the Minor Prophets, be sure to understand its audience, historical context, and literary form. Grab a Bible commentary and Bible dictionary that details each book to understand what to look for before you start to read.

Since the Prophetic Books are not presented in chronological order, it may be helpful to locate a timeline of Israel and Judah's captivity and exile to clearly understand the sequence of events the prophets wrote about. An internet search with the words "timeline of Israel's captivity and exile" or "timeline of the Old Testament prophets" will yield some solid resources.

PASSAGES TO PONDER

Jeremiah 29:11 – "For I know the plans I have for you," declares the Lord, "plans to prosper you and not to harm you, plans to give you hope and a future."

Daniel 3:17–18 – If we are thrown into the blazing furnace, the God we serve can deliver us from it, and he will deliver us from Your Majesty's hand. ¹⁸ But even if he does not, we want you to know, Your Majesty, that we will not serve your gods or worship the image of gold you have set up.

Amos 5:24 – But let justice roll on like a river, righteousness like a never-failing stream!

Jonah 2:2 – He said: "In my distress I called to the Lord, and he answered me. From deep in the realm of the dead I called for help, and you listened to my cry."

Micah 6:8 – He has shown you, O mortal, what is good. And what does the Lord require of you?

To act justly and to love mercy and to walk humbly with your God.

Bible Study Process

† Who wrote these books? Who are the subjects of these books?

† What type of books are these?

† When were these books written?

† When did the events described in the books occur?

† Where were these books written? Where do the described events take place?

† What was the historical context for these books?

† What happens within the pages of these books? What are their themes?

† Why were these books written? What are their purposes in the biblical canon?

† What did these books mean to the original audience?

† What do these books mean to us today—and to me?

† How will you respond to the truth that's been revealed to you during your study?

Major Prophets Study Questions

† Just like there are types of poems within the Psalms, there are types of prophecies within the prophetic books. Can you identify some of the common types of prophecies?

† In each book, how specifically are the children of Israel failing to keep the covenant?

† How are Isaiah and Jeremiah's prophecies similar and different?

_____
_____
_____
_____
_____
_____
_____
_____
_____

† Reading Lamentations, what can you tell about the author's perspective on the exile, and what can you learn from his perspective?

_____
_____
_____
_____
_____
_____
_____
_____
_____
_____

† At times God asks Ezekiel and other prophets to speak and perform symbolic actions to illustrate their messages. What symbolic actions do Ezekiel and the other major prophets take in their respective books and how do these actions amplify the messages?

_____

_____

_____

_____

_____

_____

_____

_____

_____

† The book of Daniel is divided between stories about Daniel's visions and Daniel in captivity. What's the benefit of showing both in one book?

_____

_____

_____

_____

_____

_____

_____

_____

_____

_____

Minor Prophets Study Questions

† Why is there so much poetry throughout the Prophetic Books, and what is its impact?

† According to Amos and Hosea, what are all the ways the Northern Kingdom has violated the covenant?

† According to Joel, Micah, Nahum, Habakkuk, and Zephaniah, what are all the ways the Southern Kingdom has violated the covenant?

† 'The Day of the Lord' is mentioned throughout many of the major and minor prophets, especially throughout Joel and Zephaniah. What is the meaning and significance of this term and why is it described in numerous books?

† What is the significance of the repeated message of most of the minor prophets warning of destruction, the need for repentance, and the promise of restoration?

† Throughout the Major and Minor prophets, God uses Israel and Judah's enemies to punish them and then punishes those same enemies. The book of Jonah, however, shows God promising to save Israel's enemies, if they repent. What does all of this reveal about God's character?

THE NEW TESTAMENT

The New Testament

The Gospels

THE GOSPELS

Matthew
Mark
Luke
John

Gospel means "good news." The four gospels—Matthew, Mark, Luke, John—named after their respective authors, present the most complete picture of Jesus's life, ministry, and death. The four books often describe the same story in different ways. The details sometimes vary, but their core message—that Jesus is the promised Messiah and Son of God—is presented throughout each.

Some skeptics argue that the differences between the four gospels discount their authenticity. However, many scholars argue that their distinctiveness proves their authenticity and divinity. "It is precisely their distinctives that are the reason for having four gospels in the first place," write authors Gordon D. Fee and Douglas Stuart in "How to Read the Bible for All Its Worth" (p. 141). Each gospel fulfills a specific purpose.

The first three books are known as the Synoptic Gospels because they are so similar. In their book, Fee and Stuart argue that Mark wrote his gospel first, based partly on his memories of the apostle Peter's preaching, and that Luke and Matthew used Mark's manuscript as the source material for theirs. "John wrote independently of the other three, and thus his gospel has little material in common with them. This, we would note, is how the Holy Spirit inspired the writings of the Gospels." (Fee and Stuart, p.142)

The Gospels consist of Jesus's life and words. In Mark 1:15 Jesus essentially sums up the four gospels: "'The time has come,' he said. 'The kingdom of God has come near. Repent and believe the good news!'"

Each gospel showed Jesus performing miracles, being accepted by many and rejected by just as many, especially religious leaders. The Gospels reveal Jesus's transfiguration high on a mountain, as well as his famous Sermon on the Mount where he declares "Blessed are the poor in spirit" (Matthew 5:3). Each gospel also showed Jesus being tried, crucified, and resurrected.

Matthew, one of Jesus's twelve disciples, wrote his gospel to a Jewish audience. Old Testament prophecies had said that the Messiah would come through the line of David. To illustrate that Jesus was truly Immanuel ("God with us"), Matthew began the book by listing Jesus's lineage, from Abraham to David to Joseph. Then he told Jesus's birth story, which also fulfilled prophecies. Matthew described many of Jesus's miracles and wrote that when Jesus healed diseases and commanded demons, he was fulfilling what the prophet Isaiah said the Messiah would do in Isaiah 53. "This was to fulfill what was spoken through the prophet Isaiah: 'He took up our infirmities and bore our diseases'" (Matthew 8:17).

Like Matthew, Mark was an eyewitness to Jesus's life, even though he wasn't one of the twelve disciples. Mark wrote his gospel to a Gentile audience to show the upside-down nature of the Kingdom of God. One story aptly sums up the Gospel of Mark. After Jesus overheard his disciples arguing about which one of them was the greatest, Jesus replied "You know that the rulers of the Gentiles lord it over them, and their high officials exercise authority over them. Not so with you. Instead, whoever wants to become great among you must be your servant, and whoever wants to be first must be your slave—just as the Son of Man did not come to be served, but to serve, and to give his life as a ransom for many" (Mark 20:25b-28).

Luke, an evangelist and companion to Paul the apostle, wrote his gospel to a Gentile audience. Many scholars believe it's the first part of Luke-Acts. A noted historian, Luke wrote the gospel to Theophilus, an unknown believer. Luke's gospel, unlike the others, went into details about Jesus's childhood. For example, in Luke 2:32, he wrote how a prophet named Simeon declared the baby Jesus "a light for revelation to the Gentiles" (Luke 2:32). Like the other gospels, Luke shared the details of Jesus's miracles, persecution, death, and resurrection. But Luke's gospel differs from the others because it documents Jesus's ascension to heaven.

The book of John is credited to John the apostle, but there's a debate about its intended audience. Some scholars say it was written to a mostly Gentile audience while others say it was written to a Jewish and Gentile audience. The book describes two of Jesus's most famous miracles, not listed in any other gospels: the wedding at Cana (John 2:1-11) and Jesus raising Lazarus from the dead (John 11). In the Old Testament, God revealed himself by saying "I AM WHO I AM" (Exodus 3:14). Similarly, throughout his gospel, John introduces Jesus through seven "I AM" statements Jesus makes.

John, like the other gospels, pens his book for one reason: "But these are written that you may believe that Jesus is the Messiah, the Son of God, and that by believing you may have life in his name" (John 20:31).

HOW TO READ THE GOSPELS

When reading Jesus's saying, keep in mind that he uses parables, proverbs, poetry, hyperbole, metaphors and the like to convey truth. Literal interpretations to all his words will leave you confused and maybe eye-less! (See Matthew 18:9.)

When reading each of the gospels, always remember that you're reading one of four separate but related accounts. Although each gospel is a complete work, collectively they tell a story as well.

PASSAGES TO PONDER

John 3:16 – For God so loved the world that he gave his one and only Son, that whoever believes in him shall not perish but have eternal life.

John 1:1 – In the beginning was the Word, and the Word was with God, and the Word was God.

Matthew 11:28 – Come to me, all you who are weary and burdened, and I will give you rest.

Matthew 28:18–20 – Then Jesus came to them and said, "All authority in heaven and on earth has been given to me. [19] Therefore go and make disciples of all nations, baptizing them in the name of the Father and of the Son and of the Holy Spirit, [20] and teaching them to obey everything I have commanded you. And surely I am with you always, to the very end of the age."

Mark 10:45 – For even the Son of Man did not come to be served, but to serve, and to give his life as a ransom for many.

Mark 12:30 – Love the Lord your God with all your heart and with all your soul and with all your mind and with all your strength.

Mark 16:15 – He said to them, "Go into all the world and preach the gospel to all creation."

Luke 4:18 – The Spirit of the Lord is on me, because he has anointed me to proclaim good news to the poor. He has sent me to proclaim freedom for the prisoners and recovery of sight for the blind, to set the oppressed free.

Luke 19:10 – For the Son of Man came to seek and to save the lost.

Bible Study Process

† Who wrote these books? Who are the subjects of these books?

_____
_____
_____
_____
_____
_____
_____
_____
_____
_____
_____

† What type of books are these?

_____
_____
_____
_____
_____
_____
_____
_____
_____
_____

† When were these books written?

† When did the events described in the book occur?

† Where were these books written? Where do the described events take place?

_____
_____
_____
_____
_____
_____
_____
_____
_____

† What was the historical context for these books?

_____
_____
_____
_____
_____
_____
_____
_____
_____
_____
_____

† What happens within the pages of these books? What are their themes?

_____
_____
_____
_____
_____
_____
_____
_____
_____

† Why were these books written? What are their purposes in the biblical canon?

_____
_____
_____
_____
_____
_____
_____
_____
_____

† What did these books mean to the original audience?

_____
_____
_____
_____
_____
_____
_____
_____
_____
_____
_____

† What do these books mean to us today—and to me?

_____
_____
_____
_____
_____
_____
_____
_____
_____
_____
_____

† How will you respond to the truth that's been revealed to you during your study?

Study Questions for the Gospels

† Why retell the same story? What unique perspective does each gospel provide?

† How does Matthew's gospel, written for a Jewish audience differ from Mark and Luke, written to a non-Jewish audience?

† Think of Jesus as an orator and storyteller. How and why does he use literary devices (parables, metaphors, similes, hyperboles, etc....) to teach?

† What are the basic elements of the New Covenant as presented in the Gospels?

___

† In Luke 4:17-18, Jesus walks into the synagogue and reads a scroll from the prophet Isaiah. How does Jesus live out these verses throughout the Gospel of Luke?

___

† What do Jesus's "I AM" statements made in the book of John reveal about his identity?

† How are the Gospels "good news"?

The Historical Book (Acts)

The Book of Acts, also known as 'The Acts of the Apostles,' is credited to Luke, one of the church's earliest historians, who was born sometime between CE 1 and CE 16. Many scholars consider Acts to be the sequel to the book of Luke, also written by Luke. Scholars estimate Acts was written between CE 60 and CE 100. The Book of Acts—like the book of Luke—is written to Theophilus, an unknown believer, but Acts is categorized as a historical book.

Acts begins after Jesus's resurrection from the dead. At the beginning of the book Jesus gathers his disciples in Jerusalem and gives them a commandment before he leaves them again: "Do not leave Jerusalem, but wait for the gift my Father promised, which you have heard me speak about. For John baptized with water, but in a few days you will be baptized with the Holy Spirit" (Acts 1:4b-5).

After this, Jesus's disciples ask him when their physical kingdom will be restored, but he responds by continuing to state how the kingdom of God will expand through the Holy Spirit once he leaves. In Acts 1:8, he says: "But you will receive power when the Holy Spirit comes on you; and you will be my witnesses in Jerusalem, and in all Judea and Samaria, and to the ends of the earth."

The Book of Acts shows Acts 1:8 in action. The book depicts how the baptism of the Holy Spirit gave believers a newfound power and new "tongues." These tongues enabled believers to proclaim the works of God in diverse world languages, and the Holy Spirit's power propelled the gospel message throughout Jerusalem, to its surrounding region, and beyond.

Peter is a central figure throughout the first part of the book. The book shows how an early church community sprouted and grew; as well as how it managed conflict within the church between different groups—including Jewish believers and Gentile believers. The book shows how church leaders worked through cultural differences to ensure that everyone's needs were being met and to avoid burdening Gentile converts with Jewish traditions. Acts shows how the gospel spread westward into the Gentile world, and how many Gentiles eagerly accepted the message of Jesus's death and resurrection. The Book of Acts ends with Paul taking the gospel message to Rome.

The book's themes include but aren't limited to community, unity, cultural intelligence, rejection, persecution, gospel expansion, and the Holy Spirit's power.

How to Read the Book of Acts

The stories in Acts show how the gospel message spread throughout and beyond the church in Jerusalem. One overacting question to keep in mind while reading is: Are the stories in Acts descriptive or prescriptive? Meaning, does Acts simply describe what happened or prescribe what should always happen? In other words, is what happened throughout the book just one possibility among many possibilities available to churches today? Considering this question will help you better understand the book and its implications for today.

PASSAGES TO PONDER

Acts 1:8 – But you will receive power when the Holy Spirit comes on you; and you will be my witnesses in Jerusalem, and in all Judea and Samaria, and to the ends of the earth.

Acts 2:1–4 – When the day of Pentecost came, they were all together in one place. [2] Suddenly a sound like the blowing of a violent wind came from heaven and filled the whole house where they were sitting. [3] They saw what seemed to be tongues of fire that separated and came to rest on each of them. [4] All of them were filled with the Holy Spirit and began to speak in other tongues as the Spirit enabled them.

Acts 2:38 – Peter replied, "Repent and be baptized, every one of you, in the name of Jesus Christ for the forgiveness of your sins. And you will receive the gift of the Holy Spirit."

Acts 16:31 – Believe in the Lord Jesus, and you will be saved—you and your household.

Bible Study Process

† Who wrote this book? Who are the subjects of this book?

_____
_____
_____
_____
_____
_____
_____
_____
_____
_____

† What type of book is this?

_____
_____
_____
_____
_____
_____
_____
_____
_____
_____

† When was this book written?

_____
_____
_____
_____
_____
_____
_____
_____
_____

† When did the events described in the book occur?

_____
_____
_____
_____
_____
_____
_____
_____
_____

† Where was this book written? Where do the described events take place?

_____
_____
_____
_____
_____
_____
_____
_____
_____
_____

† What was the historical context for this book?

_____
_____
_____
_____
_____
_____
_____
_____
_____
_____
_____

† What happens within the pages of this book? What are its themes?

† Why was this book written? What is its purpose in the biblical canon?

† What did this book mean to the original audience?

_____
_____
_____
_____
_____
_____
_____
_____
_____
_____
_____
_____

† What does this book mean to us today—and to me?

_____
_____
_____
_____
_____
_____
_____
_____
_____
_____
_____
_____

† How will you respond to the truth that's been revealed to you during your study?

Study Questions

† What does the Holy Spirit do throughout the Book of Acts?

† How, where, and to whom does the Gospel spread in Acts?

The New Testament

The Letters

THE LETTERS

- Romans
- I & II Corinthians
- Galatians
- Ephesians
- Philippians
- Colossians
- I & II Thessalonians
- I & II Timothy
- Titus
- Philemon
- Hebrews
- James
- I & II Peter
- I, II, & III John
- Jude

The New Testament letters, also known as the Epistles, include twenty-one letters written by five authors. Paul the apostle authored thirteen letters—the Pauline Epistles—including those written to churches (Romans, 1 Corinthians, 2 Corinthians, Galatians, Ephesians, Philippians, Colossians, 1 Thessalonians, 2 Thessalonians) and those written to individuals (1 Timothy, 2 Timothy, Titus, Philemon). The remaining letters, known as the General Epistles, were authored by James, Peter, John, and Jude.

One noteworthy point about the Pauline Epistles is that Paul wrote some of them while imprisoned for preaching that Jesus is king. It's also worth mentioning that Paul penned many of these letters to churches he had planted and to people he had discipled. Some letters were written to correct and encourage; Others were written to compliment and encourage. All were written with rich love and affection.

All of Paul's letters point its listeners and readers to Jesus Christ: his life, his resurrection, and how he was the fulfillment of the Torah, the Law. The Letters teach that Christ's followers receive a new identity and thus a new way of living. For example, Paul repeatedly stressed that the old social hierarchy was dismantled through Jesus. "There is neither Jew nor Gentile, neither slave nor free, nor is there male and female, for you are all one in Christ Jesus," he wrote in (Galatians 3:28). Similarly, in Colossians, 3:11 he wrote, "Here there is no Gentile or Jew, circumcised or uncircumcised, barbarian, Scythian, slave or free, but Christ is all, and is in all." Through Christ, they were all adopted sons (and children) of God. Christians of different genders, ethnicities, lineages, and social positions were all one.

Many of the Pauline Epistles addressed divisions in the various churches, including cultural differences. For instance, many Jewish Christians insisted that newly-converted Gentile believers adhere to the Torah, which mandated male circumcision and eating kosher foods—while Paul insisted that this wasn't necessary. In Romans and Galatians, Paul wrote that the Torah had been written to *show* humanity its sin while Jesus had died to *free* humanity from its sin. Redemption through Jesus, then, was enough.

Conversely, arguments abounded about which parts of the Greco-Roman culture believers could participate in and which were off limits. Could believers eat food offered to idols? Sleep with temple prostitutes? The topic of sexual immorality was discussed repeatedly throughout the Epistles. "Do you not know that your bodies are temples of the Holy Spirit, who is in you, whom you have received from God? You are not your own; you were bought at a price. Therefore, honor God with your bodies" (1 Corinthians 6:19-20).

Paul repeatedly urged the churches to honor God and to honor each other. In lieu of the Law, they could follow the Holy Spirit and receive the fruits of the Spirit. "But the fruit of the Spirit is love, joy, peace, forbearance, kindness, goodness, faithfulness, gentleness and self-control. Against such things there is no law" (Galatians 5:22-23).

Throughout The Letters, Paul also called out false teachers and false teaching. He quoted from the Old Testament and spoke of the importance of living by the Scriptures. "All Scripture is God-breathed and is useful for teaching, rebuking, correcting and training in righteousness, so that the servant of God may be thoroughly equipped for every good work" (2 Timothy 3:15-17).

A dominant and final theme in the Pauline Epistles was suffering. Some believers looked down on Paul's imprisonment and poverty, yet Paul countered by writing, "For to me, to live is Christ and to die is gain" (Philippians 1:21). In 1 and 2 Timothy, Paul advised Timothy to be ashamed neither of him nor the Gospel. Instead, Paul urged Timothy and the churches to suffer like Jesus had suffered and as Paul was suffering.

The General Epistles stressed similar themes. Hebrews, written by an unknown author, emphasized Jesus's superiority to everyone and everything: angels, priests, sacrifices, and kings. In his letter, James implored listeners to devote their whole lives to Jesus and his teachings. Like Paul, he wrote that suffering would refine them. He offered very practical advice too: "Do not merely listen to the word and so deceive yourselves. Do what it says" (James 1:22).

Peter wrote to believers that were being persecuted. In 1 Peter, he wrote that they were Christ's new temple and that they would be in exile until they reached their home in heaven. Peter stressed that enduring suffering and loving their enemies is how they would bear witness to the resurrected Christ. In 2 Peter, he wrote against false preachers that contradicted what Paul and other leaders preached.

Jude and 1, 2, and 3 John also rebuked false teachers and false teaching. "But, dear friends, remember what the apostles of our Lord Jesus Christ foretold. They said to you, 'In the last times there will be scoffers who will follow their own ungodly desires.' These are the people who divide you, who follow mere natural instincts and do not have the Spirit" (Jude 17-19).

Collectively, the General Epistles and the Pauline Epistles emphasize Jesus as the fulfillment of Old Testament prophecies; illustrate how Christ's teachings intersect with and challenge culture; show the new life through Christ; and promote unity among believers. The Letters are dense, yet rich in truth and encouragement.

HOW TO READ THE LETTERS

When reading The Letters, it's important to remember they were written for a specific reason, to a specific group of people in a specific place. Sometimes, even after researching, you still won't always understand the specifics of what was happening. That's okay. What's most important is that you always ask: What teachings apply to the original listeners of the letters, and which apply to the worldwide church today? Some parts of the letters apply to all Christians, regardless of time and culture. Other parts of the letters apply specifically to the Christians they were written to.

Reading the New Testament Letters aloud in one setting *will enable you to hear its message similarly to how its original listeners did.*

PASSAGES TO PONDER

1 Corinthians 13:4–7 – ⁴ Love is patient, love is kind. It does not envy, it does not boast, it is not proud. ⁵ It does not dishonor others, it is not self-seeking, it is not easily angered, it keeps no record of wrongs. ⁶ Love does not delight in evil but rejoices with the truth. ⁷ It always protects, always trusts, always hopes, always perseveres.

Romans 1:16–17 – For I am not ashamed of the Gospel, because it is the power of God that brings salvation to everyone who believes: first to the Jew, then to the Gentile. For in the Gospel the righteousness of God is revealed—a righteousness that is by faith from first to last, just as it is written: "The righteous will live by faith."

Galatians 2:20 – I have been crucified with Christ and I no longer live, but Christ lives in me. The life I now live in the body, I live by faith in the Son of God, who loved me and gave himself for me.

Philippians 4:13 – I can do all this through him who gives me strength.

2 Timothy 3:16–17 – All Scripture is God-breathed and is useful for teaching, rebuking, correcting and training in righteousness, so that the servant of God may be thoroughly equipped for every good work."

Hebrews 12:2 – Fixing our eyes on Jesus, the pioneer and perfecter of faith. For the joy set before him he endured the cross, scorning its shame, and sat down at the right hand of the throne of God."

Bible Study Process

† Who wrote these books? Who are the subjects of these books?

† What type of books are these?

† When were these books written?

† When did the events described in the books occur?

† Where were these books written? Where do the described events take place?

† What was the historical context for these books?

† What happens within the pages of these books? What are their themes?

† Why were these books written? What are their purposes in the biblical canon?

_____

_____

_____

_____

_____

_____

_____

_____

_____

_____

† What did these books mean to the original audience?

_____

_____

_____

_____

_____

_____

_____

_____

_____

_____

† What do these books mean to us today—and to me?

† How will you respond to the truth that's been revealed to you during your study?

Study Questions

† What are the main arguments each author makes and how does he craft each argument?

† What is the difference between having faith in Jesus and following the Torah?

† How does suffering for the Gospel shape believers and testify to Jesus?

† How can believers show love and unity when they have different ethnic and cultural practices?

† If believers' bodies are the temple of the Holy Spirit, then what actions are permitted and prohibited?

† How does Christ's reordering of social hierarchies affect the church's view of people, particularly its view of men and women?

Revelation (The Book of Vision)

Revelation was penned by a man named John, although it's unclear whether it was John the disciple or a different John. He wrote the book while exiled by the Roman government on the island of Patmos (in what's now Greece) for preaching about Jesus. Revelation is arguably the most misunderstood and hotly debated book of the Bible. The book crosses genres. It is prophetic, meaning that the author wrote about things which were yet to come. The book is also apocalyptic, meaning it portrays the end of the world. While apocalypse is a form of literature that was common in Jewish and Christian texts around the first and second centuries, it's not as common today, which makes it more challenging to comprehend. Revelation also contains letters written to seven churches in Asia Minor around the first century. Prominent themes in the book include persecution, good vs evil, judgment, justice, and newness.

John starts the book by writing that the Holy Spirit instructed him to write the letters: "Write, therefore, what you have seen, what is now and what will take place later Revelation 1:19)." Like the other letters in the New Testament, these letters offer correction and comfort. John encourages the churches who are experiencing persecution to persevere, and he rebukes those who are engaging with the immorality of their respective cultures. These letters warn of harsh punishments for those who ignore them and great rewards for those who heed them.

With its vivid descriptions of dragons, plagues, and blood, the book carries the gravitas of Old Testament prophecies and speaks to their impending fulfillment. Throughout the book, John depicts a triumphant Jesus returning to save his bride (the church) from sin and its devastating consequences on humanity and the Earth. "I saw heaven standing open and there before me was a white horse, whose rider is called Faithful and True. With justice he judges and wages war," John writes in Revelation 19:11.

Revelation is an account of the final battles—both physical and spiritual—that take place in the world before it ends. The book spoke of the future fall of the Roman Empire (which happened in 476 CE) and the demise of all empires and people that oppose Jesus's reign, including the antichrist. The book ends with Jesus "making all things new" (Revelation 21:5): a new Eden, heaven, a new Jerusalem, a new earth, and a new heaven.

When reading, look for symbolism, imagery, and their meaning. Study cryptic language to unpack their hidden meaning. Be on the lookout, also, for images from ancient mythology and the Old Testament. Next, pay attention to how the events of Revelation fulfill Old Testament prophecies and promises from God to his church. Lastly, as always, study so that your mind and heart are refined. "He who has an ear, let him hear what the Spirit says to the churches" (Revelation 2:7a).

How to Read Revelation

When reading Revelation, understand that sometimes some of the details are presented to collectively paint a picture instead of inviting a laborious interpretation of those details. In other words, you don't always need to understand all the specifics if you understand the whole picture. When in doubt, turn to trusted study resources and lean on the wisdom of scholars who've dedicated decades to studying the Scriptures.

PASSAGES TO PONDER

Revelation 1 – "I am the Alpha and the Omega," says the Lord God, "who is, and who was, and who is to come, the Almighty."

Revelation 7:9–10 – After this I looked, and there before me was a great multitude that no one could count, from every nation, tribe, people and language… ¹⁰ And they cried out in a loud voice:

"Salvation belongs to our God, who sits on the throne, and to the Lamb."

Revelation 21:1–4 – Then I saw "a new heaven and a new earth,"[a] for the first heaven and the first earth had passed away, and there was no longer any sea. ² I saw the Holy City, the new Jerusalem, coming down out of heaven from God, prepared as a bride beautifully dressed for her husband. ³ And I heard a loud voice from the throne saying, "Look! God's dwelling place is now among the people, and he will dwell with them. They will be his people, and God himself will be with them and be their God. ⁴ 'He will wipe every tear from their eyes. There will be no more death'[b] or mourning or crying or pain, for the old order of things has passed away."

Bible Study Process

† Who wrote this book? Who are the subjects of this book?

_____
_____
_____
_____
_____
_____
_____
_____
_____

† What type of book is this?

_____
_____
_____
_____
_____
_____
_____
_____
_____

† When was this book written?

_____
_____
_____
_____
_____
_____
_____
_____
_____
_____

† When did the events described in the book occur?

_____
_____
_____
_____
_____
_____
_____
_____
_____
_____

† Where was this book written? Where do the described events take place?

_____
_____
_____
_____
_____
_____
_____
_____
_____
_____

† What was the historical context for this book?

_____
_____
_____
_____
_____
_____
_____
_____
_____
_____
_____

† What happens within the pages of this book? What is its theme?

† Why was this book written? What is its purpose in the biblical canon?

† What did this book mean to the original audience?

† What does this book mean to us today—and to me?

† How will you respond to the truth that's been revealed to you during your study?

Study Questions

† How are the events described in Revelation fulfillment of Old Testament prophecies?

† Which prophecies have already taken place, and which ones have yet to take place?

NOTES